Dunster Castle

Somerset

National Trust

From fortress to family home

Over the past thousand years, Dunster has developed from a Norman fortress into a comfortable Victorian country house. Set high on the Tor from which it takes its name, Dunster has been home to eighteen generations of the Luttrell family since 1405. The Luttrells made Dunster a centre of local life – a place for polo matches and charity balls – and they also left their mark on the village of Dunster and on the huge agricultural estate that supported life in the castle. A series of four 18th-century views of this varied and beautiful landscape, which hang in the Morning Room, reveal how much has changed and how much stayed the same.

Making Dunster and making do

In times of prosperity, the Luttrells have remodelled and redecorated Dunster in the latest style:

- Sir Hugh Luttrell's outer Gatehouse of 1420

- George Luttrell's Jacobean house of 1617

- Colonel Francis Luttrell's grandly carved staircase of 1682

- George Fownes Luttrell's comprehensive Victorian modernisation of 1868–72.

(Right) Dunster Castle from the Lawns

(Below) A view of Dunster from the south-east in the late 18th century by William Tomkins (Stair Hall)

When money was short (for example in the early 18th and early 19th centuries), they sold the family silver and settled for a quieter life, but they managed to hold on to the castle through the bad times. And although Luttrells no longer live at Dunster, they still maintain their long links with this part of west Somerset, with their equally ancient home at East Quantoxhead.

Making history

Dunster may seem a somewhat remote place, cut off from the outside world by Exmoor, the Quantocks, the Brendon Hills and the Bristol Channel. But the castle and its owners have played their part in some of the most dramatic episodes in British history. The castle was besieged during the Middle Ages by King Stephen and in the Civil War, after which its fortress walls were largely demolished. In 1688 Francis Luttrell raised a regiment (later the Green Howards) to support William of Orange's attempt to overthrow James II. Luttrells set out from Dunster to fight on the battlefields of Waterloo and Normandy. The family also dominated local politics, regularly returning one of Minehead's two MPs. Portraits of Luttrells abound in the castle, putting a face to history.

Dunster today

The castle today remains much as it was in its bustling late Victorian heyday, after the architect Anthony Salvin had remodelled the building to emphasise Dunster's medieval origins and accommodate a large family and their many servants.

Key dates

	At Dunster		In Britain
Before 1066	Hill-fort occupied by Saxon Aelfric	1066	William the Conqueror becomes King of England
11th century	Castle built by William de Mohun		
Early 13th century	Gateway to Lower Ward built	1216	Henry III becomes King at the age of nine. Reigns for 56 years
1376	Dunster bought by Elizabeth Luttrell from Joan de Mohun		Edward III nears the end of his long reign
1420	Gatehouse built by Sir Hugh Luttrell		Henry V marries Catherine of Valois, daughter of King of France
1617	William Arnold builds new house		Sir Walter Ralegh leads expedition in search of South American gold
1645	Dunster besieged by Parliamentary army		Battle of Naseby
1650	Medieval fortress demolished by order of Parliament		Charles II crowned King by the Scots
1688	Francis Luttrell raises regiment to support William of Orange		William deposes James II
1815	Capt. Francis Luttrell wounded at the Battle of Waterloo		
1868	Anthony Salvin begins rebuilding Dunster		Disraeli becomes Prime Minister for the first time
1943-4	Castle used as convalescent home for war wounded		British Army fighting in Italy
1949	Geoffrey Luttrell sells the estate		Clothes rationing ends
1954	Castle and environs sold back to Luttrell family		
1976	Dunster passes to the National Trust		Severe summer drought

The Norman castle

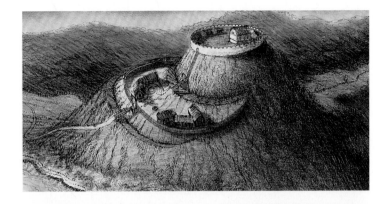

By the 15th century, a stone keep and gatehouse had been built in the Lower Ward

In 1617 William Arnold builds a new house on the site of the keep

In the early 18th century, a summer-house and bowling green were built on the top of the Tor

Tour of the Castle

The Outer Hall

Salvin created the Outer Hall in 1870–1 by sweeping away three rooms and the mezzanine floor above. A remnant of the original linenfold panelling can be seen in the small oratory off the Hall. As a result, it is higher than the Inner Hall beyond. The compartmented plasterwork ceiling and wooden fireplace overmantel are Salvin's Victorian interpretation of the Jacobean style in which William Arnold had remodelled the castle in 1617.

In 1910 the room boasted a stuffed polar bear; sadly, this has long since disappeared. In the 1930s, Alys Luttrell used this space for hosting balls in aid of the many good causes she supported.

Furniture

The octagonal table-top was originally the sounding board from above a pulpit in Wells Cathedral, where it would have helped to project the preacher's voice to the congregation.

The ash bobbin armchair and the two smaller examples nearby were turned on a lathe in the 16th or 17th century. They were inspired by medieval originals, like that in Hereford Cathedral, which were highly prized at the time. *The two high-backed, x-framed armchairs* were made about 1830, incorporating Flemish carvings of about 1600 illustrating the Passion of Christ. *The finely carved chest* is late 16th-century.

Pictures

The portrait of Oliver Cromwell recalls Dunster's troubled role in the Civil War, when the castle changed hands several times. In 1650 Cromwell ordered his troops to demolish this key strong-hold. The great medieval walls were pulled down, but fortunately the order was rescinded before the house and the gateways could be levelled. The then-owner, George Luttrell, who was sympathetic to Parliament, swore allegiance to the Commonwealth. Cromwell was sufficiently impressed to appoint him Sheriff of Somerset in 1652.

The Drawing Room

Enter through the door in the corner for a first look at this room. For a full description please refer to p.24.

Return to the Outer Hall and pass through the arches at the far end of the room to reach the Inner Hall.

(Right) *The Outer Hall*
(Left) *An ash bobbin armchair in the Outer Hall*

The Inner Hall

This was originally the Great Hall, the core of the early 17th-century house. All that survives from this period are the 'spider's-web' ceiling and the fireplace overmantel, which bears the coats of arms of Thomas and Margaret Luttrell, whose son George built the house. The animal on the crest is an otter – a pun on the family name, from the French word for a little otter: 'loutre'. The Latin motto means 'gained by strength, held by skill'. In the 1870s Salvin inserted the 13th-century-style stone chimney-piece below, having removed the 18th-century classical decoration of the room, which he considered out of keeping in a Jacobean house. The carved inscription comes from the Domesday Book entry for Dunster, and means 'the land of William de Mohun', who built the first castle. Sea shells were packed under the floorboards to dampen the noise of dancing.

Pictures

Peter Mews, Bishop of Winchester (1619–1706), to the right of the fireplace, devotedly supported the King in the Civil War, during

Salvin's Inner Hall fireplace incorporates an early 17th-century heraldic overmantel

which he was wounded on the cheek (the scar is covered by a black patch, which is turned proudly towards us). He was secretly in contact with the exiled Charles II during the Commonwealth, and was rewarded for his loyalty with a bishopric.

The religious allegory on the far wall features *Sir Thomas Copley* (d. 1584), who was Sir John Luttrell's son-in-law. He is shown with his wife Catherine and their five sons and four daughters. The central section represents the journey of the soul from earth to heaven. The devil tries to tie it down, while death cuts the thread of life with his scythe.

Go through the door beyond the fireplace on the left to reach the Dining Room.

(Right) Peter Mews, Bishop of Winchester (Inner Hall)

The portrait of Sir John Luttrell (1518/9–51) is one of the most unusual and puzzling of all Tudor images. It may refer to the peace treaty of 1550, by which France recovered the port of Boulogne from England (the woman at the top left holding an olive branch probably represents Peace). Luttrell had helped to capture Boulogne in 1544 and seems to have opposed its return – hence his shaking fist. He also fought in the bitter Scottish campaigns of the same war, during which he was taken prisoner and ransomed. The storm-tossed ship may be the *Mary of Hamburg*, which was badly damaged in the evacuation of Inchcolm Island in the Firth of Forth, where Luttrell commanded a small fleet. The Latin inscriptions on the rock and bracelet praise his courage and steadfastness. This is a copy of Hans Eworth's 1550 original (now in the Courtauld Institute in London), made in 1591 for Sir John's nephew, George Luttrell.

The Dining Room

This room was created in the 1680s as a comfortable family parlour and dining room off the Great Hall. In 1691 it was richly furnished with 21 chairs upholstered in 'turkey-work' (an English version of Persian pile carpet) and two side-tables with tops of veined black marble.

Plasterwork

The date 1681 in Roman numerals on the ceiling (over the fireplace) records the year it was put up by Colonel Francis Luttrell and his wife, Mary Tregonwell. His coat of arms appears over the fireplace, her crest in the frieze over the door to the Servery. The plasterwork has the swagger and richness of the finest late 17th-century work. Indeed, it is almost certainly by Edward Goudge, who was praised in 1690 as 'ye beste master in England in his profession'. The material is lime plaster stiffened with horse hair. The sections of repetitive ornament would have been precast in moulds, but the more complex elements were modelled freehand and *in situ* around wooden armatures. It was highly skilled and backbreaking work.

Pictures

Over the fireplace are *oval portraits of Francis Luttrell and his wife Mary*. Francis had inherited Dunster in 1670 at only eleven. So his mother ran the estate until he came of age in 1680, when he promptly married Mary, who was a wealthy heiress. Mary's money helped to pay for the creation of this grand room and for their lavish wardrobe. Mary's accounts for 1681–3 record no less than £428 spent on new clothes, including much fine lace like that which Francis wears in his cravat.

(Right) Colonel Francis Luttrell and his wife, Mary Tregonwell, who commissioned the plasterwork ceiling in this room in the 1680s

Francis is shown in armour, as befitted a colonel of the Somerset militia. However, he refused to commit his soldiers in 1685, when the Duke of Monmouth tried to overthrow James II and was defeated at the nearby battle of Sedgmoor. Francis grew increasingly disenchanted with the King and in 1688 raised a regiment at Dunster to support William of Orange, who had landed an army at Torbay to seize the throne. The uniform of his new

The Dining Room with the Servery beyond

regiment (now the Green Howards) was originally blue and yellow – the Luttrell livery.

Furniture

Early 18th-century mahogany side-tables flank the fireplace. Reddy-brown mahogany was being imported from Jamaica by the 1660s and soon became the cabinetmaker's favourite wood, because it is so hard and stable. It darkens with age. Opposite is *a late 18th-century sideboard* decorated with a 'panache' of five ostrich feathers (the Luttrell crest).

Silver

The epergne (table-centre) on the dining-table would have held fruit, sweetmeats and spices. It was made by Thomas Powell in 1780 and is engraved with the Luttrell crest.

The Servery

This small panelled room was created at the same time as the Dining Room and has a matching plasterwork ceiling. Here the Luttrells would have withdrawn after meals with a few of their most favoured guests for quiet conversation or to enjoy the many small paintings they seem to have hung on the walls.

The room was converted into a library in the mid-18th century, and in the 1870s into a more practical servery, where trays of food brought up from the new kitchen could be put down for a moment before they were served out.

The mid-18th-century chimneyboard of a flower painting was a decorative way of hiding the empty grate when it was not in use

Visit the Pantry Lobby and the Butler's Pantry (New Kitchen), then return to the Inner Hall and cross to the Stair Hall.

The Stair Hall

The oak and elm staircase was inserted in the 1680s within the medieval tower. The glory of the room is the balustrade, which was probably carved by Edward Pearce the Younger, one of the most accomplished sculptors of the age in both wood and stone. Pearce was responsible for the very similar staircase at Sudbury Hall in Derbyshire.

Each of the panels is carved from a single plank of elm 23 cm thick, and together they form a continuous rhythmic pattern of curling acanthus leaves that carries the eye effortlessly up the stairs. Running in and out of the acanthus are hunting scenes: a fox hunt, beagling and stag hunting. The carving can be dated by the Charles II silver shillings represented in the third panel up the stairs, which were issued in 1683–4. Also represented are Portuguese (with a swallow), Irish (harp) and Turkish (crescent) coins. A trophy of arms in the top balustrade commemorates Colonel Luttrell's military career.

The stairs would originally have looked rather different, as they were early on painted grey, with the coins picked out in silver leaf. Salvin stripped them back to the bare wood in the

1870s. The plain panels around the outside of the staircase were originally painted with similar acanthus ornament.

Furnishings

Below the stairs is *a display case* containing objects collected by the Luttrells over the centuries. In 1691 the room contained a map of the world and a pair of games tables complete with pieces. In 1741 there were a mahogany harpsichord, eight cane chairs, a barometer and an old tin speaking-trumpet.

The piano was bequeathed in 1996 by Vivian Ellis, composer of operettas and such popular songs as *Spread a little Happiness*.

Plasterwork ceiling

This is contemporary with the plasterwork in the Dining Room. The long panels pick up the hunting theme of the balustrade. In 1977 the ceiling was cleaned to remove centuries of grime and repainted.

In the 18th century, the windows were framed with frilly plasterwork in the Bristol Rococo style, which sat somewhat awkwardly with the robust 17th-century ceiling plaster-work. Salvin removed it in the 1870s.

Pictures

The finely dressed young man was painted in 1638 by Edward Bower. We know his age – 24 – but not his name. He is wearing 'Spanish hose' – long black breeches trimmed with bobbles and lace – and fashionably creased boots. The portrait is said to have come to Dunster in the late 19th century from Nethway, the Devon home of Henry Fownes Luttrell. Bower is thought to have trained with Van Dyck, the greatest painter of the age, and went on to paint Charles I just before his execution in 1649 (version now at Antony in Cornwall).

The view of Dunster from the south-east was painted in 1768 by William Tomkins, who also painted a series of views of Saltram in Devon. On the top landing hangs a copy of one of

The carved balustrade includes Charles II silver shillings

Murillo's beggar boy paintings, which were very popular with British collectors in the 18th century.

The Landing

The thick stone internal wall dates back to Arnold's house of 1617. The space was redecorated by Henry Fownes Luttrell in 1772–3, when the mahogany doors were put in. The classical style of the doorcase ornament is in marked contrast to the bold carving of the balustrade. It includes hunting horns and stags' heads.

Hunting imagery in a doorcase on the Landing

The Morning Room

The Luttrells' new staircase was doubtless meant to lead up to an equally impressive first-floor reception room, but lack of money or Francis's early death in 1690 seems to have brought work to a halt before it could be completed. Certainly, this room is modest after the grandeur of the Dining Room and the Stair Hall.

In 1772 Henry Fownes Luttrell made this into a breakfast room, although it was a long way from the kitchen. The chimneypiece, doors and cornice date from this period. In the Victorian era it was decorated with a green and gold wallpaper. By 1976 the paper had become so tatty that it had to be taken down. A fragment can be seen on the wall to the left of the entrance door. This became the Morning Room after Salvin's remodelling and was used as a family sitting room for the next 100 years with a Broadwood piano introduced in 1910. It was enjoyed by Alys Luttrell from 1920 until she died in 1974.

A new sofa and armchairs evoke the informal atmosphere in which visitors can sit and read more about Dunster.

Pictures

Over the fireplace is *an early 18th-century view of the south front*, showing the castle before the 19th-century alterations. In the centre of the façade is the chapel designed by Sir James Thornhill in 1722, which was demolished by

Alys Luttrell

One of the staff described her as 'a very distinguished looking lady; tall, erect, with an aristocratic face. She was strong willed and could be autocratic at times, but also extremely kind and generous and she never put on airs.' Like her husband, she was very active in local organisations such as the Minehead hospital and the Dunster Nursing Association, and enjoyed entertaining at Dunster. She was a knowledgeable gardener and accomplished rider, and in her later years, when crippled by rheumatism, one of her favourite pastimes was to drive herself around the garden in a little electric 'chariot' (as she called it), pursued by her two dogs.

The view from the castle over Dunster village in the early 18th century

Salvin in 1868 (see p. 30). All that survives from it is Thornhill's altarpiece painting of *Moses and the Brazen Serpent*, which is now in Dunster church.

The four early 18th-century paintings of the surrounding countryside make an interesting comparison with the views that you can take in from the Morning Room windows today. As you stand by the windows, you can appreciate how thick the castle walls are.

Ceramics

The Worcester dessert service, mostly of about 1770–80, is decorated with the Earl Manvers pattern. A full set would have comprised 43 pieces. The high-quality lead glaze has not crazed over the years.

The Wisteria Bedroom

The room is named after the wisteria that climbs up the wall outside the window.

George Fownes Luttrell was one of nine and he had five young children of his own, when he inherited Dunster in 1867. By contrast, the two previous owners had both been bachelors. So he had an urgent need for more bedrooms for his family and visiting relations, which he commissioned Salvin to provide. This was one of the main guest bedrooms in the Victorian castle.

The wallpaper is late 19th-century. The room has lost its original furniture, but was refurnished and reopened in 1988 by the National Trust. The wash-basin was installed in the 1930s.

Furniture

The bed is an early 19th-century four-poster with red plush pelmets and curtains. The silk counterpane was embroidered in the late 18th century by Mary Drewe, who married John Fownes Luttrell in 1782. Another panel worked to the same design is displayed in the corridor outside.

The East Quantoxhead Bathroom

The East Quantoxhead Suite

Bathroom

A glance around the door to your left reveals one of the few WCs on this floor.

Before plumbing was introduced in the 1870s, the family would have washed in their bedrooms in a portable hip-bath or at a wash-stand with a ewer and basin. Servants would have had to carry both hot and cold water up to the bedrooms by hand – an exhausting task.

The room still has its 17th-century floor-boards. It was modernised in the 1870s by Salvin, who installed the present cast-iron bath, nickel taps and mahogany surround. But it was then still the only bath in the castle. Salvin also added the Torquay red-marble fireplace.

Bedroom

This room is named after the Luttrells' other Somerset estate, where they have lived since the 13th century and continue to do so. It is one of

The East Quantoxhead Bedroom

the bedrooms modernised in the 1930s, when Geoffrey and Alys Luttrell came to live at Dunster. They had to make do with fewer servants than before, and so put in the smaller and more efficient coal-burning grates to supplement the Victorian central heating. Making up and keeping in the fires was one of the most time-consuming domestic chores in a large house.

Furnishings

Only *the dressing-table* and *the curtains* survive from the 1930s. The iron and brass bed with a half-tester canopy was brought in from another room in the castle. *The colourful patchwork quilt* was made about 1830 by Mary Drewe's three spinster daughters. It was bought back for Dunster in 1993. The wall-paper, carpet and other contents were added by the Trust.

Boudoir and Dressing Room

Completing Salvin's designs for the suite, these rooms were used for dressing, and as an informal sitting room to relax in during the day.

The Leather Gallery

In Jacobean Dunster, this was part of the Long Gallery, which may have extended into the room at the far end. In 1691 it was hung with eight paintings and a set of twelve tapestries – typical decoration for such an important space.

By 1704 it had become a formal banqueting room and continued to be used in this way until the 1870s, when Salvin remodelled the room, altering the positions of some of the doors and windows. He also rehung the leather panels, which are the chief fascination of the room today. The fine suite of late 18th-century English mahogany seat furniture is shown in this room in Victorian photographs.

Wall-hangings

Leather hangings were often chosen for dining rooms, as they did not retain the smell of stale food to the same extent as tapestries.

The panels tell the love story of the Roman general Antony and the Egyptian queen

Antony receives Cleopatra in Italy; from panel 3 of the leather hangings

Cleopatra, a story made famous by Shakespeare. Running *clockwise* from the entrance door, the scenes are as follows (the narrative order is given in brackets afterwards):

1 *The Death of Antony and Cleopatra* (6)
(Right) Antony stabs himself. (Left) Cleopatra commits suicide by clasping a poisonous snake to her bosom.

2 *Antony arms himself* (4)
Antony prepares to do battle with Octavius.

3 *Antony receives Cleopatra in Sicily* (2)
Cleopatra's golden barge is on the right.

4 *The Battle of Alexandria* (5)
Antony and Cleopatra flee after their army is defeated by Octavius.

5 *The Triumvirate (fragment)* (1)
Octavius Caesar (later the Emperor Augustus), Lepidus and Antony become joint rulers of Rome. They later fall out.

6 *Antony grants Cleopatra authority over Phoenicia, Cyprus and Judaea* (3)

The technique of decorating leather in this way was developed in Moorish Spain in the 13th century. Cordoba became the centre of the trade. Panels of calf skin or cattle hide 90 × 80 cm were first pasted together and covered in silver leaf, which was then burnished. The design was outlined on the silver leaf, and key highlights were hand tooled. The figures were then painted in oils by several different craftsmen.

(Right) The Triumvirate (panel 5)

The principal scenes were probably made in the Netherlands in the late 17th century. The floral borders were added later. They were first hung at Dunster at some point between 1705 and 1741, and were treated like grand wallpaper, being cut up and shuffled about to fit the available wall space. Not surprisingly, therefore, they were already in need of repair by 1759.

The King Charles Bedroom

This bedroom takes its name from the future
Charles II, who, as Prince of Wales, slept here
in 1645, when trying to raise support for the
Royalist cause in the West Country. Perhaps
as a result, it is said to be the most haunted
room in the castle. The warming pan was made
for his visit and is inscribed 'God Save King
Charles'. Behind the bed is a short hidden
passage which family history recounts led

to a secret ladder that would allow a quick
escape.

In the late 17th century, this was one of the
main bedrooms in the castle, furnished with a
gold-coloured bed, a suite of japanned furniture
and a set of tapestries. It seems to have been
frequently redecorated in the 18th century: in
1705 it was called the White Chamber, in 1741
the Yellow Chamber and 1781 the Red
Chamber.

Wallpaper

This is a replica of the pattern that was here in Victorian times, printed in 1991 by Perry & Coles from the original blocks. It was made originally by the Crace decorating firm to a design by A.W.N. Pugin, who masterminded the decoration of the new Houses of Parliament in the 1840s.

Furnishings

The bed and window curtains and the window seats were made up from a set of late 19th-century curtains.

Return to the Leather Gallery and take the Oak Staircase down to the ground floor.

The Oak Staircase

This was Dunster's secondary staircase, on the north side of the castle. The balusters incorporate two different designs, dating from the early 17th to the 19th centuries.

Pictures

On the east (right-hand) wall hang twelve of William Hogarth's famous mid-18th-century satires. On the north (far) wall are four scenes from Shakespeare by Henry William Bunbury.

Turn right at the bottom of the stairs to reach the Library Passage. The Billiard Room and the Gun Room are on your right.

Overmantel

The plasterwork panel over the fireplace depicts *The Judgement of Paris*. The Trojan prince Paris was asked to choose which of three goddesses was the most beautiful. He awarded the prize – a golden apple – to Venus after she had promised him the love of any woman he liked. His choice of Helen sparked off the Trojan Wars.

The panel was moved from another room in the castle and today it sits somewhat awkwardly over the much smaller chimney-piece. Dated 1620, it was made by a team of itinerant craftsmen active in the West Country. Like many such plasterwork scenes, it was based on a Flemish engraving, in Jacob Floris's pattern-book of 1566.

The Billiard Room

The Gun Room

The Gun Room was another part of Salvin's modern, Victorian 'male' suite of rooms with the Office, Billiard Room and Library. This functional, bustling space would have been used by servant and master; staff cleaned, serviced and stored guns which were picked up and dropped off by family and guests. It was also a convenient drop-off for luggage.

Blood sports have always been popular on country estates and at the turn of the century Dunster was a 'sporting paradise for a boy … when one was promoted to a gun in the holidays; there was every variety of game to shoot on non-hunting days'. This included woodcock, blackgame, pheasants, partridge, golden plover and snipe.

In the 1920s and 30s, Geoffrey Luttrell's enthusiasm for shooting kept the Gun Room busier than ever. It remains very unaltered since then. The room's dull green 'masculine' colour

The Billiard Room

No Victorian country house was thought to be complete without a billiard room, where one could wile away an empty evening or a wet afternoon. It was generally a male preserve, but by the late 19th century many women also played.

Salvin created this room in the 1860s out of what had formerly been the kitchen. He retained the fireplace arch, but placed a much smaller grate within it. Salvin also reinstalled here the late 17th-century doors and doorcases that he had removed from the Dining Room and Inner Hall. The two 18th-century Corinthian columns once formed part of the screen that divided the Stair Hall and Inner Hall. They now flank a leather sofa, from which one could watch play.

The wallpaper, which was put up in 1977, is a faithful reproduction of the Victorian pattern that was here before.

Furnishings
The billiard-tables and accessories were made by Burroughs & Watts Ltd, the most famous Victorian maker of billiard-tables.

Salvin reinstalled the 1680s carved doorcases in his new Billiard Room

(Above) The Gun Room

has been repainted and original fixtures kept: such as the fitted cupboards, deerskin leather straps, gun racks, and an armoire which was probably converted for use as an additional gun rack. There is a shotgun that visitors can handle.

The muskets on the walls date from an earlier Dunster Armoury. Colonel Francis Luttrell collected 43 of these muskets when he led the local militia in the 1670s and 80s. Some still bear his initials 'FL'.

The Library Passage

A door on the right is labelled 'Muniment Room No. 1'. This is one of two rooms designed by Salvin to store the extensive Luttrell archives. The family papers survived the upheavals of the Civil War, having been reorganised in 1650 by the pamphleteer William Prynne, who had found them in 'confused chaos'. In the early 20th century they were recatalogued by the family historian Sir Henry Maxwell Lyte, and

have been on deposit in the County Record Office in Taunton since 1958.

Pictures

The walls are hung with some of the many views of Dunster Castle and village, and the surrounding landscape.

Walk to the far end of the passage and look right into the Justice Room.

The Justice Room

This room was also created by Salvin out of an old scullery. George Luttrell used it as his office, but also his private retreat for rest and relaxation during the day. Here he would interview tenants and estate staff, who would be let in via an outside door in the passage. From 1848 Justices of the Peace could no longer hear cases at home, but the term remained in use.

Across the passage, directly opposite the Justice Room, is the Library.

The embossed wallpaper in the Library features hoopoes

The Library

Salvin created this room in 1870–1 out of three smaller rooms and the mezzanine floor above. He designed the oak bookcases and furnished the room with comfortable maroon leather chairs and settees (now protected from light damage by case covers).

The Victorian 'Cordelova' pattern wallpaper is embossed in imitation of Spanish leather hangings like those displayed in the Leather Gallery upstairs.

Ceiling plasterwork

Salvin's Jacobean-style ribbed ceiling retains its original colouring, which is subtly related to the wallpaper.

Pictures

The portraits include three owners of Dunster between 1867 and 1957.

To the left of the fireplace is *George Fownes Luttrell* (1828–1910), who inherited Dunster from his uncle in 1867 and commissioned Salvin to rebuild this room and much of the rest of the castle. He was a calm, unselfish and slightly diffident man, but he could speak out when he thought it necessary. He disliked gossip. His fascination with the past encouraged him to excavate medieval Cleeve Abbey and to rebuild

Dunster in medieval style. He was a strong supporter of the Liberal Prime Minister, Gladstone, but, unlike many of his ancestors, was never an MP.

To the right of the fireplace is *his wife, Anne Elizabeth Hood* (1829–1917), whom he married in 1852. She was descended from Admiral Hood, who gave his name to the battleship sunk by the *Bismarck* in 1941.

Over the door is *their son, Alexander Fownes Luttrell* (1855–1944). In his youth he served in the Grenadier Guards in the Sudan. His coming-of-age in 1876 was marked with great celebrations at Dunster, although he was absent on military service. He inherited in 1910 and devoted the rest of his life to the estate, despite preferring to live at East Quantoxhead rather than at Dunster, which was left empty until 1920. Appropriately, he was buried in a coffin made from an ancient oak from the park.

Over the fireplace is Alexander's son, *Geoffrey Fownes Luttrell* (1887–1957). From 1914 he served in Australia as private secretary to his

Anne Elizabeth Hood, who, with her husband, George Fownes Luttrell, commissioned this room; painted by Cyrus Johnson

The Library

uncle, who was Governor-General. He wanted to join the army, but was found unfit for military service. To improve his health, he chose an outdoor life, working for a year as a fisherman off the coast of Victoria. He returned to Britain in 1920 and settled at Dunster, which once again became the centre of local life after a period when the house had been empty. He became an expert breeder of Dorset Horn sheep. In 1949 he decided to sell the estate to a property developer on condition that it was kept together. After this undertaking was reneged on, he managed to buy back the castle in 1954.

Books

There has been a library at Dunster since at least the late 17th century, but very little of its contents survives here. One exception is

Richard Crakanthorpe's *Logica* (1677), which was used by Alexander Luttrell when he was a student at Cambridge in the early 1680s. There are numerous late 17th- and 18th-century Bibles and prayer books, which may have been used in the Thornhill chapel (now gone), and also a Bible inscribed as for use in the Housekeeper's Room in 1846. Otherwise, it is a very miscellaneous collection, typical of country houses with long histories and fluctuating fortunes. It includes a run of the 18th-century *Racing Calendar*. The collection was given to the National Trust by Sir Walter Luttrell in 1992.

The most famous book associated with the family is the early 14th-century Luttrell Psalter (now in the British Library), which is illuminated with intimate images of medieval life. It was commissioned by a Lincolnshire forebear, Sir Geoffrey Luttrell. There is a Victorian edition in the Dunster library.

The Conservatory

Cheaper iron, glass and coal encouraged many Victorians to add conservatories to their homes. They were often placed, as here, next to libraries, offering a contrast of natural light, colour and scent to the gloom and tobacco smoke of such rooms. In July the perfume of jasmine and geraniums permeates the house, and a mass of smaller pot-plants trail from the hanging baskets and wirework stands. The terracotta floor tiles are Minton.

'This luxury of conservatories added to rooms and opening into them has become general – enlivening old thick-walled mansions as well as new built boxes.'

Maria Edgworth, 1820

The Drawing Room

This forms the ground floor of the great tower that Salvin added to the south front. It is deliberately unsymmetrical, with large and small bay windows, where quiet conversations could be held in some privacy. In the late 19th century, the family took tea here every afternoon at 5; in fine weather, they would move to the terrace. The Luttrells would also receive local gentry paying social calls in this room. It was not much used again until 1935, when Alys Luttrell revived it as a formal drawing room.

Salvin designed the neo-Jacobean ceiling, the frieze of which incorporates the initials 'GFW' for George Fownes Luttrell, who commissioned the room. Somewhat surprisingly, he also chose the chimneypiece, which is in a very different, late 18th-century style. Much of the 18th-century furniture in this room was here by 1910. The grandest piece is the large ebony cabinet of

The Conservatory

The Drawing Room

*c.*1860 against the far wall, which is decorated with ormolu (gilt bronze) mounts and *pietra dura* (hardstones).

Salvin's decoration was much altered in the 1930s, when it was painted the present shade of green. However, his elaborate parquetry floor, with its geometric inlay, has survived.

Photographs

On the table are photographs of Alys Luttrell, the last member of the family to live at Dunster, and of her son, Walter, on the day of his wedding to Hermione Gunston, on 23 December 1942.

(Right) The neo-Jacobean frieze in the Drawing Room incorporates the initials of George Fownes Luttrell, who created the room

Lighting

Salvin installed *the brass gasolier*, which may have been designed by Pugin and which was later converted to electricity. Gas was originally generated by a plant in the basement.

Return to the Conservatory, and leave by the outside door in this room to reach the garden.

The Garden

Dunster may have been built as a fortress, but since the 18th century its steep slopes have increasingly been given over to gardening. This lofty spot is vulnerable to winter gales, but because of its coastal position enjoys a mild climate, and frosts are rare. The views from the garden are the special glory of Dunster. They are as varied as they are panoramic, taking in meadow and moorland, deer-park and wood-land, the waters of the Bristol Channel and the rooftops of Dunster village.

Turn right out of the Conservatory, and walk along the south front and climb up to the Keep Garden on the Tor.

The Tor

The highest point on the property was the site of the Upper Ward of the medieval castle. Its remains were levelled in the early 18th century to make a bowling green, beside which the octagonal summer-house was built. By 1830 the slopes below were covered with evergreens, flowering shrubs and trees, including laurustinus (*Viburnum tinus*), which is still to be seen here, having spread widely by self-seeding. Other features are the Rose of Sharon and the Lesser Periwinkle. The east–west path leads to the Pets' Cemetery, last resting-place for many of the family's favourite animals, including Kirstie (1939–47), a dog who was the 'beloved companion and comfort' of Alys Luttrell.

The reservoir (now empty) was built in 1870 as a fire precaution and to provide water pressure for the castle and the village.

The South Terraces

A series of terraces clings on to the precipitous hillside to the south of the house. Two rectangular flower-beds were laid out here, which were later gravelled over. Sheltered from the prevailing winds and rain, the sandy loam soil here is often hot and dry, making a friendly habitat for sun-loving, tender plants. The most famous of these is the Dunster lemon, which has been growing against the castle walls since at least 1830, protected in winter by its own glasshouse. This has recently been rebuilt with the generous support of local National Trust Associations and donations from visitors. Among the other plants that

The Bucks' engraved view of the garden in 1733, showing the Gatehouse on the right and the octagonal summer-house recently built on the top of the levelled Tor

The mild microclimate of the garden supports palm trees and other tender plants

flourish in these arid conditions are mimosas, Chusan palms, cordylines, yuccas, hypericum, buddleja, *Beschorneria yuccoïdes* and *Correa speciosa*.

The Gatehouse and Tenants' Hall

From the Green Court in front of the castle you get a good view of the folly built by Richard Phelps for Henry Fownes Luttrell in 1775 on top of neighbouring Conygar Hill. Luttrell spent £4 2s 6d keeping the builders supplied with cider.

The path back to the car-park passes the Gatehouse, which was built about 1420 by Sir Hugh Luttrell. The upper storey was remodelled in 1764 and again in 1871–2 by

Salvin, who created the spacious Tenants' Hall. Here the tenant farmers would come to pay their quarterly rent, and meetings, feasts and other celebrations would be held. Today, it provides the setting for weddings and special events.

(Right) The Gatehouse

The Stables

Horses have always been an important part of Dunster life. Before the motor car, they drew almost every load that came to the castle up the steep drives. They also carried the Luttrells over their huge estates and on the hunting and polo fields.

The present stables were built in the 17th century. They are an important early surviving example and must have been very grand when in full use. In the first stalls in the long west range you may see rare early hanging partitions, called bales. The oldest stall divisions in the west range were originally a red-brown colour but later layers of paint show shades of yellow ochre used throughout the stables. A shiny varnish possibly made the paint more resistant to knocks and easier to wash down.

The shorter north range houses the National Trust shop. In 2008 the plaster ceiling and walls were restored in here and the woodwork redecorated to match one of the historic colours. Both ranges could have looked like this in their prime from the 18th century, right through the time that Salvin was redesigning the castle and into the early 20th century.

The Luttrells' passion for horses continued but the stables fell out of general use by the 1930s as they were not easily converted into the larger 'loose boxes' preferred. Horses were stabled in Dunster village instead but occasionally visiting polo ponies were still bedded down in this historic interior.

The stables house an exhibition about the history of Dunster and the people who have lived and worked here.

Take the path south from the west end of the drive along the bank of the River Avill.

The Castle Mill

There has been a water-mill at Dunster since at least 1086, when the Domesday Book recorded two here. Medieval estates made much use of such mills, where manorial tenants were obliged to grind their corn on pain of heavy punishment.

This mill was rebuilt in its present form in 1779–82, when new French millstones and machinery were installed. By the 1930s it had become more picturesque than productive. It was refurbished in the 1940s and continued grinding corn until 1962. Mr A. S. Caps, a National Trust tenant, put it back into working order in 1979.

The nearby two-arch Lovers' Bridge was built in the 18th century by Richard Phelps for Henry Fownes Luttrell. The banks are a perfect habitat for moisture- and shelter-loving plants, such as hydrangeas, hostas, ferns and *Gunnera manicata*, and for specimen trees.

The Castle Mill

The Deer-park

From the castle you get good views south over the 18th-century deer-park (which is not National Trust property).

Dunster has had its own deer-park since medieval times, but it then lay to the north-east at Marshwood near Blue Anchor. In 1755 Henry Fownes Luttrell decided 'to bring the park home' by creating a larger deer-park of 348 acres (141ha) to the south of the castle. This entailed removing the tenants, grubbing up the medieval hedges and building a new wooden perimeter fence. The villagers were then recruited to drive the herd of fallow deer from Marshwood along a specially made route to Dunster. Henry Fownes Luttrell planted many of the mature trees in the park as cover for his deer and game, although some date back to the Middle Ages. At the same time, he constructed a new road along the line of the present A39.

In the early 20th century, a polo ground was laid out in the flat meadows to the east of the River Avill, an area now known as the Lawns. Among those who played here was the Maharaja of Jodhpur (whose kingdom in Rajasthan gave its name to a type of riding breeches). In 1928 the Maharaja brought a crack team and a string of 62 polo ponies by special train for a match against the West Somerset Polo Club.

After the Second World War, the Grand Western Archery Society requested use of the Hanger Park for an annual tournament. Alys Luttrell was appointed as Lady Paramount for the tournament, which still takes place and is the largest archery competition in the West of England. The Luttrell connection continues with Lady Hermione Luttrell as Lady Paramount.

The Maharaja of Jodhpur's polo team at Dunster in 1928

Architectural history

The medieval castle of the Mohuns

The original Norman fortress was built on two levels – the Upper Ward on the Tor, the Lower Ward below what is now the Green Court. The first, probably timber and earth fortifications were replaced in stone in the early 12th century. The oldest surviving part of the castle is the twin-towered gateway to the Lower Ward, which was built in the early 13th century by Reynold de Mohun II. Astonishingly, it still has its original iron-bound gates. A survey made in 1266 listed the rooms in the castle's Upper Ward; they included a hall, with a buttery, pantry, kitchen and bakehouse, a chapel and a prison. All have long since disappeared.

The Luttrells put their family's stamp on the place in 1420, when Sir Hugh built the outer Gatehouse above the Mohun gateway, using red sandstone brought by sea from

The white Portland stone of the new chapel stands out from the rest of the south front in this early 18th-century view

Bristol. He also reroofed the castle with 10,000 Cornish stone tiles. Dunster seems to have fallen into disrepair during the 15th and 16th centuries. When the antiquary John Leland visited in 1542, he noted, 'The dungeon [keep] of the castelle of Dunestorre hath been fulle of goodly building. But now there is but only a chapelle in good case [repair].'

George Luttrell, who inherited in 1571, repaired both the castle walls and the inside of the building (the Inner Hall overmantel is dated 1589) before embarking on a much more ambitious project.

The early 13th-century gateway to the Lower Ward

The new Jacobean house

In October 1617 George Luttrell drew up a contract with William Arnold for 'a house or parcell of building to be sett up and built within the castle of Dunster'. Arnold was to supply a plan and elevation and to oversee the work. He was a leading master-mason active in the West Country in the late 16th and early 17th centuries, and was probably the architect of Montacute, one of the great Somerset houses of the 1590s. He was also experienced in remodelling old buildings like Cranborne House in Dorset (1608–12). Arnold transformed the medieval fortress into a Jacobean H-plan country house, but managed to incorporate much of the old fabric. The north entrance front was made symmetrical, with a central entrance porch-tower, flanked by towers in the angles of the corner wings. There was very little external decoration apart from the purely ornamental battlements, which alluded to Dunster's castle history. Colour provided the main animation, the red sandstone walls contrasting with the creamy-coloured door and window surrounds.

As all too often happens, architect and client fell out. Luttrell refused to pay Arnold's fee of £40, and Arnold sued for his money. Luttrell counterclaimed that the design had been changed without his agreement, that the work done was poor, and that the cost had risen from the original estimate of £462 to over £1,200.

The house survived the Civil War sieges, but after Dunster had been captured by the Parliamentary army in 1646, the medieval walls were largely demolished on the orders of Oliver Cromwell.

The 18th-century chapel

In 1720 Colonel Alexander Luttrell's widow, Dorothy, created a less steep approach to the castle, which was christened the New Way. Three years later, she levelled the remains of the medieval Upper Ward on top of the Tor and turned the site into a bowling green. She also commissioned Sir James Thornhill to build a new private chapel against the south front. Thornhill was a Dorset man who was then reaching the end of his distinguished career as a mural painter, which had included the baroque decorations in St Paul's Cathedral and the Painted Hall at Greenwich. Sadly, no visual record was made of the chapel's interior before it was demolished in the 1860s, but we know that it was decorated with panelling, pilasters and stucco, all painted a stone colour. There were also painted festoons between the windows. It probably resembled the chapel Thornhill decorated at Wimpole Hall in Cambridgeshire. Paintings show that the outside was faced in gleaming white Portland stone, in contrast to the red sandstone of Arnold's house.

The entrance front of William Arnold's Jacobean house in 1839, before it had been remodelled by Salvin

Salvin's remodelling of the castle, 1868–72

George Fownes Luttrell chose Anthony Salvin to rebuild Dunster because of his great experience working on ancient castles such as Alnwick in Northumberland. Luttrell was anxious to respect Dunster's medieval origins and Jacobean remodelling, but little had been done to the house for a century, and he badly needed larger reception rooms for entertaining, more bedrooms for the family and for visiting friends and relations, and more up-to-date servants' quarters. Salvin's first scheme, estimated at £35,000, was rejected as too expensive. The revised plan reduced the amount of decoration, which was to be 'all plain except in the best sitting rooms'. The final bill came to £25,350; by contrast, Salvin's work at Alnwick had cost £250,000.

Salvin remodelled the symmetrical Jacobean exterior to give it a more picturesquely irregular silhouette that would match the castle's dramatic position. To the entrance front he added a new kitchen tower on the left, with an octagonal stair turret attached. He created a new entrance porch decorated with heraldry, and rebuilt the roof-top battlements. On the site of Thornhill's chapel in the centre of the rear façade he raised a huge new drawing-room tower. Inside, between the Stair Hall and the Inner Hall, he replaced an 18th-century screen of classical columns with a pair of medieval-looking stone arches, but retained the Elizabethan plasterwork ceiling. Salvin wanted his changes to look as though they had been made gradually over the past centuries, 'the walls and arches to be of the earlier date into which the style of Elizabeth has been introduced'. He inserted new, but old-looking windows for the same reason and to break up the symmetry of the Jacobean house. Salvin envisaged providing new furniture in a matching style, which he was adept at designing, but, if it was ever delivered, it does not survive at Dunster.

Salvin reorganised the servants' quarters by placing the butler's offices conveniently adjoining the Dining Room in the new Kitchen tower, with the Kitchen in the semi-basement below. He also introduced the latest domestic technology – gas lighting, central heating and running hot water by H. C. Price & Co. of London, and kitchen equipment by Stuart & Smith of Sheffield. However, not

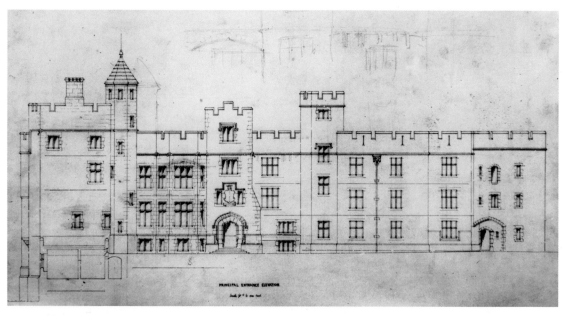

Salvin's elevation drawing for the entrance front

everything was to be made new.
As Salvin explained: 'I do not expect
or care to find suites of rooms in a
castle such as you naturally expect in
a modern house.'

The house was partly redecorated
in the 1930s, when Geoffrey and Alys
Luttrell were living here, but the
structure was altered very little during
the 20th century.

*(Right) The south front is dominated by
Salvin's central Drawing Room tower*

*(Below) Salvin added the massive Kitchen
tower to the left end of the entrance front*

Life in Victorian Dunster

The Victorian country house that Salvin created at Dunster in 1868–72 required a large staff to run it, despite all the labour-saving devices he had incorporated. The indoor servants numbered fifteen in 1881 (see panel). The head of the household was the butler, who had direct responsibility for all the male indoor staff. From the window of the Butler's Pantry, he could see visitors approaching up the drive from the Gatehouse and be ready to greet them at the front door. From his pantry, the butler could supervise the serving of food, which arrived in the adjoining Pantry Lobby by a hoist from the Kitchen on the floor below. He could also keep a careful eye on the nearby Strong Room. The menservants were responsible for serving meals and brushing down dirty outer clothes (the only method available before dry-cleaning was introduced in the late 19th century). They also cleaned and filled the oil lamps, which supplemented the gas lighting introduced by Salvin.

The housekeeper looked after the female staff and ordered groceries and other outside supplies. The housemaids cleaned the house, kept the fires in and changed the bed linen. Ladies' maids had a slightly higher status. As their name suggests, they attended female members of the family, helping them to wash and dress. In the 1870s, there were also three nursery staff to look after the Luttrells' young children. The cook's domain was the kitchen, pantries and scullery, where meals were prepared, food stored and the washing-up done. A set of spring-mounted bells in the passage outside the Servants' Hall was connected by pulleys and wires to the upper rooms,

The servants' bells outside the Servants' Hall

The household in 1871

George Fownes Luttrell and his wife Anne were in their early forties. They had four children between the ages of three and seventeen, who were looked after by a governess, nurserymaid and nurse. The head of the servants was the housekeeper, Harriett Whiteside (51). The cook, Amelia Payne, was only 21. The other house staff comprised a ladies' maid, kitchenmaid, housemaid, footman and groom – ten in all. Anne's mother, Amelia Hood, was also staying and had brought her own ladies' maid. The gardeners and other stable staff were not recorded in the 1871 census, as they lived out.

from where the family could summon assistance, when needed.

When the family was in residence, the servants were kept very busy. The housemaids got up at 5.30am to clean the principal rooms before the Luttrells came down. While the family were eating breakfast, they would make up the beds. Only then could they have their own breakfast in the Servants' Hall. The upper

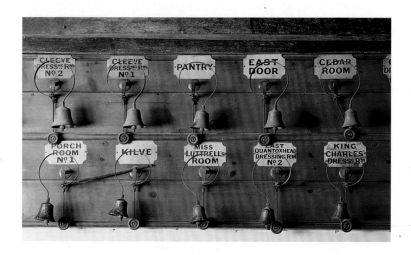

servants often ate separately in the housekeeper's room. The female staff slept in small bedrooms at the top of the Kitchen Tower, the male servants at the opposite end of the castle. Although the sexes were strictly segregated, there were still illicit night-time meetings on the Dunster battlements.

It was a hard life, and few of the junior staff stayed long. But working in a large country house like Dunster had its compensations. It was secure employment with meals and accommodation provided in comfortable and beautiful surroundings. It was also a much more sociable existence than working in a smaller house, where you might be the only servant.

The household in 1881

The staff had grown to fifteen, but as the youngest child, Beatrice, was now nineteen, the nurserymaids had gone. However, Alexander, who was a lieutenant in the Grenadier Guards, had brought his valet. The living-in staff comprised the butler, housekeeper, two footmen, a groom, a hall boy (aged sixteen), two ladies' maids, a housemaid (Caroline Webber, who was the only servant that remained at Dunster from 1871; she was still here in 1891) and six other female servants. Most were from Somerset, but one was born in Scotland – the ladies' maid Mary Ramsay.

The servants' quarters

The servants' quarters of most large Victorian country houses were placed in a separate wing, to avoid kitchen smells and the danger of fire. Salvin added a new Kitchen Tower to the north-east corner of the castle, but because of the constricted hilltop site, he had to sink most of the new domestic offices below ground, on two basement floors stretching away towards the Gatehouse. The underground position did, however, help to keep the larders cool and the servants' comings and goings out of sight.

The servants' quarters can be visited on regular guided tours. The Trust has made no attempt to replace the kitchen coppers and other utensils that have been lost. In their authentic, unrestored state, these subterranean spaces remain deeply atmospheric, recalling a complex world of service that has now completely vanished.

1 The Crypt

Deliveries of dry goods, meat and dairy produce were received here, before being taken up for storage in the larders and pantries.

2 The Coal Cellars

Coal was carried from here along a passage to the base of the Kitchen Tower, from where it could be lifted three floors by a mechanical hoist.

3 The Game Larder

The iron wall-brackets would have supported beams, from which meat, game and poultry could be suspended on butcher's hooks. Slots in the east and west walls allowed a through draught to ventilate the room.

4 The Dairy Larder

Eggs, butter, cheese and other dairy produce were stored on the slate shelves, which were cool and easy to wash. The daisy-pattern ventilation holes in the doors are a favourite Salvin motif.

5 The Scullery Passage

This connected the larders to the Kitchen. The cement skirting was impervious to gnawing rats and mice.

6 The Pastry Larder

Well away from the heat and steam of the Kitchen, this provided the ideal conditions for pastry-making.

7 The Scullery

Dirty vegetables and crockery were washed here.

8 The Kitchen

This is much larger and higher than the other rooms in the servants' quarters, to enable the great heat generated by the ranges to dissipate. The central arch still has its original Stuart & Smith roasting range.

9 The Still Room

This was the housekeeper's own kitchen, where she would prepare special preserves and make up breakfast trays for the family. The best china was stored in the glass-fronted cabinets.

10 The Drying Room

Wet clothes and dishcloths were dried here.

11 The Bell Lobby

12 The Servants' Hall

13 The Housekeeper's Room

She used this as her own sitting room, where she would take afternoon tea.

14 The Butler's Pantry

From here the butler managed the male servants, and was responsible for the silver, wines and spirits, and for service at table.

15 The Pantry Lobby

Food arrived here in a dumb-waiter direct from the Kitchen on the floor below. A speaking tube, with a whistle attached, allowed the butler to communicate directly with the cook.

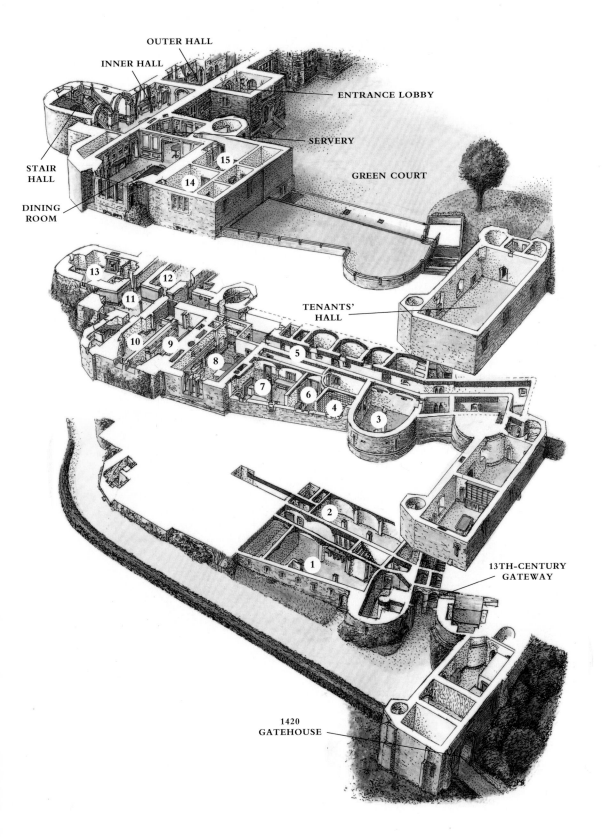

OUTER HALL

INNER HALL

ENTRANCE LOBBY

SERVERY

STAIR HALL

GREEN COURT

DINING ROOM

15

14

13

12

11

10

9

8

TENANTS' HALL

5

7

6

4

3

2

1

13TH-CENTURY GATEWAY

1420 GATEHOUSE

The owners of Dunster

The Mohuns

The Tor at Dunster commands the Avill Valley
to the south and the coast road to the north, and
so was an obvious place for a fortress. Before
1066 it belonged to the Saxon Aelfric, who built
a wooden hill-fort here. The first castle was built
by William de Mohun, one of the Norman war-
lords who came over to England with William
the Conqueror in 1066. In 1138 Dunster was
besieged by King Stephen, who was disputing
Matilda's claim to the throne, a claim supported
by the Mohuns. Matilda created the Mohuns
Earls of Somerset for their loyalty. The family
gained a reputation for good works, being active
in founding monasteries in Somerset and
Devon.

The sale of Dunster

In 1330 Sir John de Mohun inherited Dunster
while still a boy of ten. He went on to fight at
the battle of Crécy for Edward III, who
appointed him one of the first Knights of the
Garter in 1348. Sir John was a brave but spend-
thrift man, who was dominated at home by his

Sir Hugh celebrates his first Christmas at Dunster, 1405

The household accounts reveal that, on
20 December 1405, Sir Hugh spent 20d on
new trousers and shoes for two of his
servants 'because of the approach of
Christmas'. He also bought six fur-lined
gowns as Christmas presents for his wife
and their daughters. On Christmas Eve,
rushes were 'brought to strew in the hall
and the chambers'. At the Christmas feast,
the family ate venison and wine bought
in Taunton, while estate tenants played
music, and children from Minehead (who
were paid 20d) danced for them.

*The tomb of Joan, Lady de Mohun, who
sold Dunster to the Luttrells; from Charles
Stothard's* Monumental Effigies

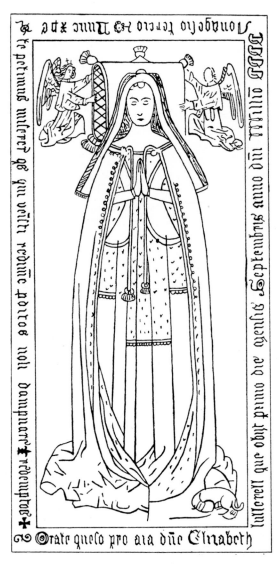

The alabaster grave cover of another Lady Elizabeth Luttrell, wife of Sir James. Married three times she had two Lancastrian husbands killed in the Wars of the Roses and Dunster Castle confiscated. She successfully petitioned Henry VII for the castle's return to her son before her death in 1493; from Henry Maxwell Lyte's A History of Dunster

wife Joan. Anxious for the future because of his growing debts and their lack of children, she was determined to take over the running of the estate. Eventually, Dunster was put in the hands of trustees, who allowed Joan to sell it in 1376 to Lady Elizabeth Luttrell for 5,000 marks. In the 14th century it was very unusual for land to change hands by sale rather than inheritance, and even more for the parties involved both to be women. The exchange did not in fact happen for another 30 years, as Joan retained a life interest in the property and outlived Lady Elizabeth, not finally dying until 1404.

The Luttrells

Like the Mohuns, the Luttrells were a Norman family and had been settled in this part of west Somerset since the early 13th century, when they acquired East Quantoxhead (which remains in the family seven centuries later).

Elizabeth's son, Sir Hugh Luttrell, finally took possession of Dunster in 1405. He renovated the castle, which was in some disrepair, and in the 1420s built the Gatehouse.

During the Wars of the Roses, the Luttrells supported the Lancastrian side. Sir James Luttrell was fatally wounded at the second battle of St Albans in 1461, and when the Yorkists temporarily gained the upper hand, Dunster was confiscated. Sir James's son, Sir Hugh Luttrell, retrieved it in 1485 on the final Lancastrian victory of Henry VII, but he preferred to live at East Quantoxhead, like many of his descendants.

Sir Hugh's grandson, Sir John Luttrell, is remembered most vividly through his unusual allegorical portrait in the Inner Hall (see p. 9). He spent much of his life at war, helping to capture Boulogne from the French in 1544 and

The tomb of Sir Hugh Luttrell, who built the Gatehouse, and his wife, Catherine Beaumont, in Dunster church

leading the attack against the Scots at the Battle of Pinkie in 1547. He died young in 1551, while planning an expedition to Morocco.

George Luttrell, builder of the house

During Sir John's frequent absences on campaign, Dunster was run by his mother Margaret. She also outlived her younger son, Thomas, who died in 1571, leaving a son and heir, George, aged only eleven. She objected strongly when George's guardian tried to marry the boy to his daughter, Joan Stewkley. Margaret thought her a 'slutte', who 'had no good qualities', and the marriage was possible only after she died in 1580. George's second wife, Silvestra Capps, seems to have been just as difficult: her second husband claimed she was greedy, unpleasant and vulgar. Despite this apparent domestic discord, George set about transforming the castle, with a new house, and the locality by building the Yarn Market in the village and the pier at Minehead.

George Luttrell, the builder of Jacobean Dunster

The Civil War

At the outbreak of war in 1642, the Marquess of Hertford marched into Somerset seeking support for the King. However, George's son, Thomas Luttrell, who backed Parliament, refused to let him into Dunster. Thomas's wife stoutly defended the castle, ordering her men to fire on the Royalists, who beat a hasty retreat to Minehead, where Thomas had disabled the fishing fleet by removing their rudders. Hertford returned the following year with a larger army, and on 7 June 1643 Luttrell surrendered. He died in 1644 and his family left the castle, which was handed over to a Royalist governor, Col. Francis Wyndham. In May 1645 Dunster played host to the fifteen-year-old Prince of Wales, who had travelled from Bristol to escape the plague, although Dunster village was also to be stricken with the disease. The bell-ringers were paid 14s in beer to welcome the future Charles II's arrival in Minehead. Six years later, Col. Wyndham sheltered Charles at Trent Hall during the King's famous flight to safety as a fugitive from the Parliamentarians.

In November 1645 the tables were turned, when the castle was besieged by a Parliamentary army under Col. Blake, who set up his artillery in the village behind what is now the Luttrell Arms Hotel. The earthworks are still visible there, and Civil War cannonballs were discovered lodged in the rafters of the castle stables, when the National Trust took on Dunster. In January 1646 Sir Thomas Fairfax arrived with more gunpowder for the explosive mines that Blake was laying under the castle walls. The next month, a royalist relieving force broke through the besiegers, bringing much-needed relief supplies. But when spring came, the siege was renewed, and prospects for the garrison again looked bleak. Wyndham negotiated an honourable surrender, and on 22 April his troops marched out with colours flying.

After the execution of Charles I in 1649, the threat of a royalist rising in the West Country gradually subsided, but Dunster Castle remained of such strategic significance that Parliament decided that it would be prudent to demolish its fortifications. The curtain walls that had stood for three centuries were reduced to rubble in twelve days in August 1650. The destruction was witnessed by the pamphleteer William Prynne, who had fallen out with both sides and was then being held prisoner at Dunster. Prynne recorded that Thomas Luttrell's son George, having retrieved his shattered inheritance, had managed to save the house and was beginning to rebuild the family fortunes: 'His wife [Elizabeth] is now pregnant. God send her a sonn and heir, a joyful delivery and numerous happy posterity.' Sadly, Prynne's prayers were not answered. The much-hoped-for son was born on 18 April 1651, but survived only three weeks, being baptised and buried on the same day. Elizabeth Luttrell herself died the following year.

Dunster revived

George's brother and heir Francis probably supported the Commonwealth, as his wife Lucy was a granddaughter of the leading Parliamentarian John Pym. But he made his peace with Charles II's new regime in 1660, becoming MP for Minehead. Like many of the Luttrell men, he died young, in 1666, leaving his wife to manage the estate and bring up their three young sons. In 1663 he had bought a child's saddle for them 'of pinck coulored plush trimed with silver lace'.

When the Luttrells' second son and heir, also called Francis, came of age in 1680, he promptly married Mary Tregonwell, an heiress worth £2,500 a year from Milton Abbas in Dorset.

The plasterwork ceiling of the Dining Room was part of Francis and Mary Luttrell's lavish modernisation of Dunster in the 1680s

The young couple had the energy and the money to start bringing the castle back to life after the disasters of the Civil War. They commissioned a new carved staircase balustrade and plasterwork in the height of fashion, and spent large sums on new furniture, silver and clothes.

Francis served as a colonel in the Somerset Militia, but played an equivocal part in the Monmouth rising of 1685 against James II. However, he became so disillusioned with the King that he decided to back William of Orange in 1688, when the Dutch ruler landed at Torbay in Devon to seize the throne. The regiment he mustered to the cause at Dunster on 19 November is today one of the most famous in the British Army – the Green Howards. Francis died young in 1690, leaving his remodelling of Dunster unfinished and his widow Mary with heavy debts. She was obliged to use her private fortune to buy the contents of the castle. She installed them in her London house, but they were destroyed when it was burnt to the ground in 1696. Mary was lucky to escape with her life, being rescued from the flames by Sir Jacob Bancks, a Swedish diplomat turned naval officer. The story has a happy ending, as they were married the same year. The couple did not live at Dunster, but Bancks commissioned the statue of Queen Anne that now stands in Wellington Square in Minehead.

The Luttrells shop for clothes in Covent Garden, August 1681	
Making a rich laced cloath suite	£1 18s
Silk and galloone [a kind of lace]	5s
A pair of scarlett silk stockings with gold	£1 15s
Buckles to the britches	3s 6d
Silk to line the britches	3s 6d
Pocketts and staying tape	3s 6d
A sett of rich gold buttons	£2 14s 6d

The 18th century: death and debt

During the first half of the century, none of the Luttrell men lived long enough or had enough money to put their mark on the place.

Dunster remained unoccupied until 1704, when, following Mary's death, it was inherited by Francis's younger brother, Alexander. The estate was still deep in debt, and the house was thinly furnished: the 1705 inventory reveals that the Little Parlour contained only two tables, 'one brush to wipe tables' and 'one Chaire for a Child'. Alexander died only six years later, leaving a six-year-old son, another Alexander, and a widow, Dorothy, who managed the estate until her death in 1723. She paid off the debts, and even found money to make some improvements to the castle, including commissioning the Thornhill chapel (see p. 31). Her son Alexander finally came of age in 1726, but died young only eleven years later, leaving yet more debts and an only daughter, Margaret, aged eleven. Dunster was placed in the hands of a receiver, who sold the family silver to pay the bills and closed up the castle.

The family returned to Dunster in 1747, when Margaret came of age and married her cousin, Henry Fownes, who added the Luttrell name to his own. It was almost a century since the last substantial changes to the interior, so the young couple set out to redecorate in the latest Rococo taste. They had sketches made for new furniture, ordered Chinese painted wallpaper, and inserted new windows in the Dining Room and the Stair Hall. Henry also reasserted the family's traditional place in local politics by getting himself elected MP

(Top right) Dorothy Luttrell, who managed the estate and commissioned the Thornhill chapel after the death of her husband, Alexander (right), in 1711

for Minehead. He had a fondness for port, which was probably responsible for the gout that afflicted his hands. Henry's funeral was a very elaborate affair, which included his empty carriage in the cortège.

His eldest son John, who succeeded to the estate in 1780, consolidated the Luttrells' land holdings in the area and indulged his love of horse-racing, winning cups at Lichfield in 1781 and Totnes in 1789.

Rococo Dunster

In the 1750s Maurice Harris supplied the Luttrells with this extraordinary sketch for a new Rococo chimneypiece in the Withdrawing Room (the room immediately above the Dining Room, not open to visitors). At the same time, Spinnage & Crompton of London put up the papier-mâché ceiling decoration in the same room, which still survives.

Henry Fownes Luttrell and his wife, Margaret (Dining Room)

The 19th century

'A sad picture of departed greatness'

John Luttrell was succeeded by another John (1787–1857), who was MP for Minehead until the seat was abolished by the Great Reform Act of 1832. He never married and seems to have preferred life in the capital. He did, however, open the castle to the public. Elizabeth Ernst recorded her husband's reaction after a visit in 1845:

The present state of the castle exhibits a sad picture of departed greatness. The owner, an inveterate bachelor, lives in London, and hardly ever comes here. Two maiden sisters live in the castle – in great seclusion – the stables containing stalls for 20 or 30 horses are quite empty and not a dog in the kennel…. The old servants, coachman, groom, huntsman, gamekeeper are retained, but have nothing to do and about 20 idle people dine together every day in the [Servants'] Hall.

John was followed in 1857 by his brother Henry, who inherited the estate at the age of 67, having also spent most of his life in London. Henry was another bachelor, and so had little need to make changes during the decade he owned Dunster.

Dunster transformed

Things changed dramatically in 1867 with the accession of Henry's nephew, George Fownes Luttrell. Agriculture was at the height of its mid-Victorian boom, and Dunster's 15,000 acres (6,070ha) were bringing in a rental income of £22,000 a year. Money also came from quarrying and forestry. George and his wife Anne had a growing young family. So they had the means and the incentive to modernise the castle, where little had been done for a century. They introduced up-to-date Victorian technology, but were keen to respect Dunster's ancient traditions. Indeed, their architect, Anthony Salvin, replaced

A witness to history

John's younger brother, Captain Francis Luttrell, was staying at Dunster in 1815, when news came that Napoleon had escaped from Elba and was marching towards Paris with a new army. Francis hastily returned to London to rejoin his battalion, the 1st Foot Guards. Before setting out for the Continent, he bought himself a new tent, camp bed, folding chairs, table and cutlery – all carefully marked with his name. Francis's battalion played a decisive part in the Battle of Waterloo, driving back Napoleon's elite Imperial Guard at a crucial moment. Francis was wounded in the eye, but survived the engagement, and his son George, who was born thirteen years later, went on to inherit Dunster. This portrait, painted in 1855, shows Francis proudly wearing his Guards uniform and Waterloo campaign medals.

much of the 18th-century decoration with medieval-style heraldry, windows and plaster-work to make the place look more castle-like (see p. 32).

George Fownes Luttrell helped to bring the outside world to this hitherto-remote area by backing the new railway line to Minehead (his son Alexander cut the first turf for Minehead station). He also developed the town as a seaside resort. Dunster village was not forgotten: he turned to the leading Gothic Revival architect G. E. Street to restore its church in 1875–7.

Luttrell's efforts received the royal seal of approval when the Prince of Wales spent two nights at the castle in August 1879.

(Right) George Fownes Luttrell, who rebuilt the castle; portrait by Cyrus Johnson in the Library

(Below) The Outer Hall in the late 19th century

45

The 20th century

In 1876 Alexander Luttrell was commissioned into the Grenadier Guards (which had been his grandfather's regiment at Waterloo). He was serving in the Sudan that year when he came of age, an event celebrated at Dunster with much ringing of church bells and firing of cannons. On his return, the village was decked with bunting, 'welcome home' banners and arches of evergreens, and a banquet was held in the castle.

Alexander helped with the running of the estates from 1890, but when he succeeded to Dunster in 1910, he preferred to live at East Quantoxhead, leaving the castle empty. However, he remained very much involved in supporting local organisations.

Alexander's son Geoffrey and his wife Alys came to live at Dunster in 1920. With their two young sons and adopted daughter, they brought

Geoffrey Luttrell; by Oswald Birley (Library)

(Far right, top) Alexander Luttrell; by Mark Milbanke (Library)

(Far right, bottom) Alys Luttrell; by Philip de Laszlo. She was the last member of the family to live at Dunster

the castle back to life once again, hosting a busy round of charity balls, dinner parties, concerts and shooting parties at Dunster. In 1943 they offered the castle as a convalescent home for wounded naval and American officers, who were welcomed like guests at a continually changing house party.

When Alexander Luttrell died in 1944, the estate was left – not for the first time in its history – deeply in debt, in this case to the taxman. Geoffrey decided, very reluctantly, that the only option was to sell up. The castle and 8,600 (3,480ha) acres of the estate were bought by the Ashdale Property Co. in 1949 on the understanding that its historic integrity would be preserved intact, with the Luttrells remaining as tenants of the castle and home farm. The Commissioners of Crown Lands subsequently acquired the estate and in 1954 sold the castle back to the Luttrells.

Geoffrey's son, Walter, who succeeded in 1957, was a keen rider, both on the hunting and the polo fields. While a student at Oxford in the late 1930s, he would rise before dawn on winter Saturdays and drive to Dunster for breakfast so that he could hunt his pack of beagles. It was natural, therefore, that he should serve in a cavalry regiment, the 15th/19th the King's Royal Hussars, during the Second World War. In 1942 he married his wife, Hermione Gunston, who later worked for the Special Operations Executive, which was running agents behind enemy lines in Europe. He won the Military Cross in the bitter tank battles of the Normandy campaign, and later joined and commanded the North Somerset Yeomanry as a TA officer. He lived at East Quantoxhead from 1951, serving as High Sheriff and later as Lord Lieutenant of his native county for sixteen years. In 1970 he was a founder member of the Wessex regional committee of the National Trust. He gave the castle and the greater part of the contents to the Trust in 1976. He was made KCVO in 1993 – the first member of the family to be so honoured.

THE LUTTRELLS OF DUNSTER CASTLE

Sir Andrew Luttrell = Elizabeth Courtenay (d. 1395)
(d. c.1380) | *buys Dunster estate 1376*

Sir Hugh† = Catherine Beaumont†
(c.1364–1428) | (d. 1435)

Sir John = Margaret Tuchet
(1394–1430)

Sir James = Elizabeth Courtenay†
(c.1426–61) | (d. 1493)

Sir Hugh = (1) Margaret Hill
(d. 1521) | (2) Walthean Yard

Sir Andrew = Margaret Wyndham*
(c.1498–1538) | (d. 1580)

Sir John* = Mary Rice   Thomas† = Margaret Hadley†
(1518/19–51) | (d. 1588)   (1525–71) | (d. 1607)

3 daus.   George† = (1) Joan Stewkley (d. 1621) m. 1580
                 (1560–1629) | (2) Sylvestra Capps (d. 1655) m. 1622

Thomas* = Jane Popham
(1584–1644) | (d. 1668) m. 1621

Alexander   George = (1) Elizabeth Prideaux (d. 1652)   Francis = Lucy Symonds
(1622–42)   (1625–55) | (2) Honora Fortescue   (1628–66) | (d. 1718) m.1655

Thomas   Col. Francis* = Mary Tregonwell*   Col. Alexander* = Dorothy Yard
(c.1657–70)   (1659–90) | (d. 1704) m.1680   (1663–1711) | (d. 1723)

Tregonwell   (1) Alexander = Margaret Trevelyan* = (2) Edward Dyke   Francis of Venn* = Anne Stucley*†
(1683–1703)   (1705–37) | (d. 1764)   (1709–32) | (d. 1731)

(1) Margaret* = Henry Fownes* = (2) Frances Bradley   Anne* = Edward Pleydell
(1726–66) m. 1747 | (1723–80) | m. 1771   (1731–1820)

Margaret* = John Henry   Alexander   John* = Mary Drewe*   Charlotte = Francis (1756–1823)
(1747–92)   Southcote   (b. + d. 1749)   (1752–1816) m. 1782 | (d. 1829)   (d. 1817) | m. 1788

John   Henry   Lt. Col. Francis = Emma Louisa Drewe   12 children
(1787–1857)   (1790–1867)   (1792–1862) | (d. 1881) m. 1824

George* = Anne Hood*   8 other children
(1828–1910) | (d. 1917) m. 1852

Alexander* = Alice Munro Ferguson*
(1855–1944) | (d. 1912) m. 1886

Geoffrey* = Alys Bridges (1884–1974)
(1887–1957) | m. 1918

Lt. Col. Sir Geoffrey = Hermione Gunston   Julian = Anne Cazenove
Walter, MC   (1923–2009)
(1919–2007)   m. 1942   Serena   Alistair

* denotes a portrait in the castle
† denotes a monument in Dunster church